YOU CHOOSE
BOOKS ™

THE HARLEM RENAISSANCE

An Interactive History Adventure

by Allison Lassieur

Consultant:
Zoe Burkholder, PhD
Assistant Professor, College of Education and Human Services
Montclair State University

CAPSTONE PRESS
a capstone imprint

You Choose Books are published by Capstone Press,
1710 Roe Crest Drive, North Mankato, Minnesota 56003
www.capstonepub.com

Library of Congress Cataloging-in-Publication Data
Lassieur, Allison.
  The Harlem Renaissance : an interactive history adventure / by Allison Lassieur.
    pages cm.—(You choose history)
  ISBN 978-1-4765-0256-4 (library binding)
  ISBN 978-1-4765-3609-5 (paperback)
1. African Americans—Intellectual life—20th century—Juvenile literature. 2. Harlem
Renaissance—Juvenile literature. 3. African Americans—History—1877-1964—Juvenile literature.
4. African American arts—20th century—Juvenile literature. 5. Harlem (New York, N.Y.)—
Intellectual life—20th century—Juvenile literature. 6. New York (N.Y.)—Intellectual life—20th
century—Juvenile literature. 7. African American intellectuals—New York (State)—New York—
History—20th century—Juvenile literature. I. Title.
  E185.6.L33 2014
  974.7'100496073—dc23   2012051694

Editorial Credits
Brenda Haugen, editor; Bobbie Nuytten, designer; Wanda Winch, media researcher;
Charmaine Whitman, production specialist

Photo Credits
©2013 Archives Center, National Museum of American History, Kenneth E. Behring Center, Smithsonian Institution, 40; AP Images, cover; Berea College, Berea, Kentucky, 70; Corbis: Bettmann, 74, 80, 84, 88, 98, 100, Labrecht Music & Arts, 94, Underwood & Underwood, 53; General Research and Reference Division, Schomburg Center for Research in Black Culture, The New York Public Library, Astor, Lenox and Tilden Foundations, 12; Getty Images/Chicago History Museum/Jun Fujita, 21, 38, Frank Driggs Collection, 72, Hulton Archive, 77, Hulton Collection, 29, Time & Life Pictures/Alfred Eisenstaedt, 42; Library of Congress: General Collections/NAACP, 48, 62, Manuscript Division/Harmon Foundation Records, 64, 66, Prints and Photographs Division, 6, 47, 58, 83, 102, NAACP Records, 56, 105; National Archives and Records Administration, 33; Newscom: Zuma Press, 11; Photographs and Prints Division, Schomburg Center for Research in Black Culture, The New York Public Library, Astor, Lenox and Tilden Foundations, 16

Source Notes
Chapter 3
Page 46, line 6: Langston Hughes. "The Dream Keeper." *Survey Graphic*, March 1, 1925, Vol 6, Issue 6, p. 664.
Page 65, line 8: Claude McKay. *Home to Harlem*. Boston: Northeastern University Press, 1987.

Printed in the United States of America in Stevens Point, Wisconsin.
032013   007227WZF13

TABLE OF CONTENTS

ABOUT YOUR ADVENTURE

YOU are living during an exciting time—the Harlem Renaissance. From music to books, the art world is flourishing. Anything seems possible.

In this book you'll explore how the choices people made meant the difference between life and death. The events you'll experience happened to real people.

Chapter One sets the scene. Then you choose which path to read. Follow the directions at the bottom of each page. The choices you make will change your outcome. After you finish your path, go back and read the others for new perspectives and more adventures.

YOU CHOOSE the path
you take through history.

COLORED
WAITING ROOM

PRIVATE PROPERTY
NO PARKING
Driving through or Turning Around

Black travelers in the South were directed to "colored only" waiting areas at bus stations.

A RENAISSANCE OF ART AND IDEAS

Something exciting is happening in the world, and you can feel it. New music, called jazz, bursts out of the radio. You're reading books by black writers. You see black teachers, doctors, nurses, and lawyers in your town. People you know are going to college! People are calling this time the "Negro Renaissance."

This renaissance may be new, but it started a long time ago. When the Civil War ended in 1865, your grandparents were slaves. After the war they were freed. Many former slaves stayed in the South. Others moved to big cities in the North.

7

Turn the page.

For a time, things were good. New laws gave black people rights they'd never had before. They could buy property, go to school, and run for political office.

Many white people didn't like these changes. Southern states started passing Jim Crow laws. It became illegal for white people and black people to go to the same schools or shop at the same stores. Black people lost many of the freedoms they had gained after the Civil War. More and more black families moved north to escape Jim Crow laws. This move came to be known as the Great Migration. One of the places they moved to was Harlem, in New York City.

World War I (1914–1918) brought more changes. Thousands of men, black and white, became soldiers. Black men had a chance to show their bravery in battle.

But there was a limit on how many black volunteers could join the Army. Fortunately factories that made war materials needed workers. Black people got some of these well-paying jobs. For the first time, many could afford to buy houses, cars, and other luxuries.

After the war black soldiers, workers, and businessmen expected that they would be treated with respect. They had fought for their country. They had worked hard in the factories for the war effort. But they faced the same racism and hatred as they did before the war. They were pushed out of their jobs. Companies refused to hire black workers. Educated black people were forced to work as maids, waiters, drivers, or in other low-paying jobs. All these things caused frustration and anger between blacks and whites.

Turn the page.

This anger burst out in the summer of 1919. Race riots broke out in big cities such as Omaha, Nebraska; Chicago, Illinois; and Washington, D.C. It was called Red Summer because of the bloodshed and death.

At the same time, many black writers, musicians, dancers, actors, and artists decided to fight racism by speaking out against it. This was the start of the renaissance.

From the end of World War I in 1918 until the early 1930s, the Harlem Renaissance gripped the world. Harlem was the center of black arts and culture. Plays performed by black actors came to Broadway. All-black orchestras made records and toured Europe. Performers such as Josephine Baker wowed audiences in the United States and abroad. Novels by black writers such as Claude McKay, Jessie Fauset, and Zora Neale Hurston became best-sellers.

You're living
in the time of the
Harlem Renaissance.
It feels like anything
is possible.

Josephine Baker sang in Paris, France. Her act was popular in Europe as well as the United States.

11

→ To be a young man who has just arrived in New York or Chicago in 1919, turn to page **13.**

→ To be a talented, ambitious writer in 1925 Harlem, turn to page **41.**

→ To explore Harlem nightlife in 1927, turn to page **73.**

Cotton was the most important crop in the South.

CHAPTER 2

MOVING NORTH

Farming is the only life you have known. You were born here in southern Alabama in 1901. Your grandparents were slaves. They purchased the farm when they were freed after the Civil War. Your dad was born here. All your brothers were born here too.

You gaze across the fields. They were once filled with cotton. Not anymore. Several years ago, the boll weevil came. The insects destroyed all the cotton for miles around. When your brothers decided to leave, Dad sadly agreed that they should try to find a better life elsewhere. The two oldest, James and John, moved to New York City. Another brother, Abraham, moved to Chicago, Illinois.

13

Turn the page.

James and John joined the Army to fight in World War I. Abraham hoped to find a job. Thousands of other black people from all over the South moved north as well. Newspapers are calling it the Great Migration. Being only 15, you were too young to leave. Now it's January 1919, you're almost 18, and the war is over.

Your town has changed since the war. "Whites only" signs are appearing all over town. People say a group of white men roam the county at night. Last month they set fire to a black farmer's barn. They said it was because the black farmer had disagreed with a white man in public. No one was arrested, even though everyone in town knew who did it.

It's not this bad everywhere. There's something new going on for black people in the world. Your brothers fill their letters with stories of how good life is in the North. They tell you about well-paying jobs and the exciting nightlife. They send you copies of newspapers, magazines, and books. The pages are filled with stories of black dancers, singers, artists, and writers. There are even black millionaires.

The sun has almost set when your father comes out on the porch. "It's time you got away from here too," he says, as if he could read your mind. "Either New York or Chicago would be a fine place to make a life for yourself." He hands you an envelope. Inside is enough money for a train ticket.

"What about you and Ma?" you ask.

"We'll be fine," Dad says with a smile.

Turn the page.

After the boll weevils, Dad planted peanuts instead of cotton. So did many other farmers. It looks like the farms will survive. But you don't want to farm anymore. The next week you tell your parents good-bye and head to the station.

In the early 1900s, 7 million black Americans lived in the South. Fewer than 1 million lived in all other regions of the United States combined.

→ To go to Chicago, go to page 17.

→ To go to New York City, turn to page 27.

The train is crowded with black people going north. Most are young men like you.

As you step off the train in Chicago, you are overwhelmed with the crowds and the noise in the busy station. Just as you wonder how you'll ever find your brother Abraham, he grabs you in a big hug. After a short bus ride, you get off in front of a large three-story building.

Abraham leads you to the second-floor apartment where he lives with two other men. The front room includes both a small kitchen and a living room. Everyone sleeps on mattresses in the back room. Suddenly you miss your narrow twin bed at home. Maybe this wasn't such a good idea after all.

Abraham sees the look on your face. "Don't worry, little brother," he says. "You'll do fine here—just you see."

Turn the page.

Six months have passed. You almost can't remember what life on the farm was like. You quickly found a job at a factory making $2 a day. That's more money than you ever dreamed of! For the first time in your life, you can eat at restaurants and go to the theater. On Saturday nights you and Abraham go to nightclubs and listen to jazz. There are plenty of pretty girls to dance with too. Now it's late July, and the city is hot as an oven.

"Let's go swimming," Abraham says one morning. "Lake Michigan will feel good on a day like today."

It sounds like a good idea. But there have been problems between blacks and whites lately. White soldiers home from World War I can't find work because black workers have filled many good jobs. Some places have fired blacks and given those jobs to whites. Other companies keep their black workers because they pay blacks less than white workers for the same jobs. White people are angry with black people for moving into their neighborhoods. Black people are angry because they still face as much racism in the North as they did in the South.

Turn the page.

Just last week, on July 19, a huge race riot broke out in Washington, D.C. It started with a rumor that a black man had attacked a white woman. Groups of white people roamed the streets, beating up black people. The police were slow to help. The black community fought back. That riot lasted four days. Fifty-four people died. Now everyone in Chicago is on edge. Maybe you should stay home today instead.

→ *To stay home, go to page* **21.**

→ *To go swimming, turn to page* **37.**

Abraham hasn't come back from the lake when you hear shouting in the streets. Outside, people are running up and down the street. "What's going on?" you shout from the window.

"A black youth, Eugene Williams, was killed by a white mob at the beach today!" someone yells back. "The police wouldn't arrest the people who killed him. Now there's a riot going on!"

People carrying bricks and stones chased a black man in Chicago.

Turn the page.

The shouting gets louder, along with the sounds of gunshots and shattering glass. A large group of white men is running down the street with guns and baseball bats. The men break down the door of a building and rush inside. Furniture starts flying out of windows. If you stay in the apartment you might get attacked too. If you leave, the mob might see you.

➤ *To stay in the apartment, go to page* **23.**

➤ *To flee, turn to page* **24.**

You lock the door and pile furniture against it. You grab a knife from the kitchen and hide under a mattress. The mob breaks down your building's door and stampedes in. Someone runs up the stairs and rattles your door. Closing your eyes, you wait for them to break the door down. But instead they clomp back down the stairs. That's when you smell the smoke. They've set the building on fire!

Smoke fills the apartment before you can get to the door. You cough as you try to move all the furniture. The thickening smoke makes it hard to see. Your lungs burn. You can't catch your breath. There's still furniture in front of the door, but you don't have the energy to move even one more thing. It's no use. You collapse and die from the smoke.

THE END

To follow another path, turn to page 11.
To read the conclusion, turn to page 101.

Quickly grabbing a knife, you climb out of the back window and jump down into the alley behind the building. From all the noise, you expect there is more than one group of white men attacking the neighborhood. There's nowhere safe you can go.

Suddenly Abraham appears. "They're burning everything," he says. "We've got to go. Follow me."

You zigzag through alleys and behind houses, staying just out of sight of the mobs. Being seen means being beaten or killed. The two of you crouch behind a building and watch your apartment burn. Everything you worked for is gone.

"Come on," Abraham says. "I have a friend who will help us." Soon you're in an unfamiliar neighborhood. Abraham heads to a tidy brick home. You can't believe it when a white man opens the door.

"Ed Dabrowski is a friend from work," Abraham tells you. "He doesn't like what is happening to Negros in the city." You eye the man suspiciously.

"Don't be afraid," Mr. Dabrowski says with a thick Polish accent. "Your brother is a good man. We have worked side by side for a long time. You're safe here."

Turn the page.

The two of you stay with Mr. Dabrowski for a week, until the riots end. The papers are filled with the terrible news. Twenty-three black people and 15 white people are dead, more than 500 injured, and hundreds of black families are homeless.

You're one of the homeless too. The factory where you work has closed because of the riots. Abraham is determined to stay, but you've had enough. A quiet life on the farm sounds pretty good now. You've saved just enough for a train ticket back home. Your part of the Great Migration is over.

THE END

To follow another path, turn to page 11.
To read the conclusion, turn to page 101.

The train ride takes only a few days. Finally you're in New York City! The huge train station is choked with smoke, crowds, and noise. For the first time, excitement turns to fear. Frantically you search the platform. You don't see John and James anywhere. Maybe they're running late. You find a seat and wait until the crowds are gone. Your brothers still haven't arrived. By now you're starving. There must be a restaurant somewhere nearby.

→ To explore New York City, turn to page **28**.

→ To wait for someone to find you, turn to page **36**.

The cold wind whips your threadbare coat as you leave the station. Huge buildings stretch into the clouds. Cars, trolleys, and carriages clatter through the streets. A small, brightly lit diner sits on a corner. The black man behind the counter smiles when you come in. He sets a steaming bowl of soup and a cup of coffee on the counter.

"I'm Albert. New to town?" he asks. Nodding, you tell him you missed your brothers. He looks at the address on the letter you brought from home.

"That's way up in Harlem," he says. "I'd like to move up there. There's music all the time, great clubs, and the parties! Up in Harlem a black man can do anything. When I came here I had nothing. I worked hard and saved money. I always wanted to own a restaurant. If I'd stayed in Mississippi, all I could be was a farmer."

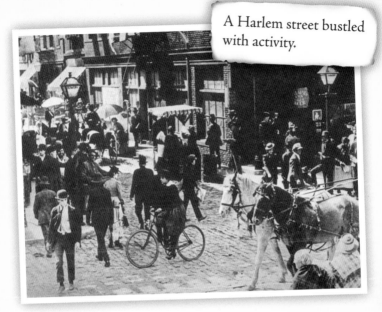

A Harlem street bustled with activity.

You tell him about the boll weevils. "The weevils took my family's farm too," he says. "Tell you what. I'll pay you to help clean up tonight and give you a place to sleep. You can head to Harlem in the morning."

You'd rather get to your brothers' apartment tonight. But you're exhausted from the travel.

→ To stay overnight, turn to page **30**.

→ To go to Harlem, turn to page **31**.

You sweep the diner's floor and wash some dishes. Then you collapse onto a mattress near the stove. The next day the diner is busy, so you stick around and help out. It's harder work than you expect. But you make $2 in tips. That's more money than you've ever had at once. Albert is impressed. "My nephew used to work with me, but he went off to war and didn't come back. Now that the war is over, business is picking up. If you want a job, you've got it," he says.

It's not what you expected to be doing, but it's a job. You can send word to your brothers about where you are. They'll be down here to get you soon enough.

THE END

To follow another path, turn to page 11.
To read the conclusion, turn to page 101.

It's tempting, but you are eager to see your brothers. "I understand," Albert says. He tells you how to get to Harlem. Then he presses a dollar into your hand. "From one southern farmer to another," he says. "Be sure and stop in the next time you're downtown."

By the time you get to Harlem, it's late. Even so, you're shocked to find the streets filled with people. Restaurants and clubs line the streets. Music floats through the air. Everyone is dressed for a party. And every face you see is black. A well-dressed man directs you to the building. When you knock on the apartment door, a stranger opens it.

Turn the page.

"You must be John and James' brother!" the woman says, pulling you into the small apartment. "My name is Faye. I'm your cousin."

That's news to you, but Faye is too happy to stop. "I'm so glad you found your way up here." Faye explains that she's staying with your brothers until her family arrives from Alabama.

"Your brothers are still with their regiment." she says. "They're staying at the Armory until the parade tomorrow."

The 369th arrived back in the United States.

The next morning there's excitement in the streets. The 369th is coming home! You know about your brothers' regiment and its bravery in France during the war. The infantry soldiers fought so fiercely they were nicknamed the Harlem Hellfighters. You could stand out on the street with Faye to watch the parade. But you'd like to see your brothers before the march.

→ To stay on the Harlem street, turn to page **34**.

→ To find your brothers, turn to page **35**.

There's no way you'll find your brothers in this crowd, so you decide to stay. When you hear the sounds of the marching band, your heart races. Dressed in their uniforms and helmets, the soldiers march in formation. Faye points out the drum major, Bill "Bojangles" Robinson. You've heard of him from your brothers' letters. He's a musician and dancer. Thirteen hundred soldiers march behind him.

There they are! "James! John!" you shout, waving. They glance toward you and grin. You're so proud of them. After the parade you'll find your brothers and start your new life in this exciting place.

Faye gives you a hug. "You're going to love it here. I'll help you find a job. Harlem is the best place in the world to be!"

THE END

To follow another path, turn to page 11.
To read the conclusion, turn to page 101.

You haven't seen your brothers in more than two years. You're not going to wait another second. You dodge the crowds as you run down Fifth Avenue. You finally see the soldiers. They've stopped for a moment. You plunge into the ranks yelling "John! James!" You hear your name and are caught in a crushing hug.

Up close you can see your brothers' uniforms are tattered and mended. Their weapons are dented and scratched. The regiment begins marching again, but now it's more casual. Friends and family march alongside their soldiers. John puts his dented helmet on your head, and you almost burst with pride. Your brothers are home, and you're in Harlem, ready to start your new life.

THE END

To follow another path, turn to page 11.
To read the conclusion, turn to page 101.

You're awakened by a shove. You must have fallen asleep. Two white police officers stand over you. "You should be up in Harlem with the rest of your kind," one officer growls. The other slams a baton over your head. Blood spurts from the wound as you fall to the ground unconscious.

When you wake, a black doctor is standing over you. "I'm Dr. Louis Wright," he says. "You're banged up, but you'll be fine." When he leaves, John and James explain that a train conductor found you and brought you to Harlem Hospital.

"You're safe now," James says. John nods. "I'm sorry you got such a bad start," John says. "But it will be great from now on." You believe them.

36

THE END

To follow another path, turn to page 11.
To read the conclusion, turn to page 101.

The water does feel great. You and Abraham swim in the water with other black people near one side of the beach. Whites swim near the other side of the beach. There are no signs or ropes keeping everyone apart. It's just understood that everyone stays on "their" side. You think it's silly that the lake is divided this way, but you don't know what to do about it.

"What's that fool doing?" Abraham says. A black teenager is swimming toward the "whites only" area of the beach. A group of white people gathers and watches. The white men start throwing rocks at the teen in the water. One rock hits him on the head. He disappears under the water. Your heart pounds as you wait for him to resurface. When that doesn't happen, you're horrified to realize that he's drowned.

Turn the page.

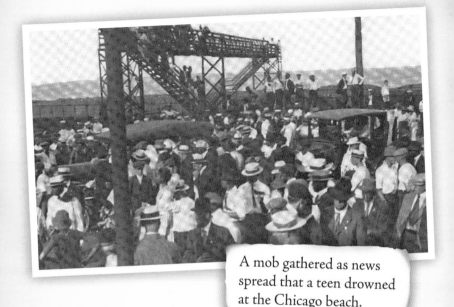

A mob gathered as news spread that a teen drowned at the Chicago beach.

You run to a white police officer near the crowd.

"Aren't you going to do something? Arrest that man! He's the one who threw the rock!" you shout. Other blacks are also pleading with the officer to arrest the murderer. The officer ignores everyone and turns away. Suddenly you find yourself in the middle of a huge fight. Fists are flying as whites and blacks attack one another.

Something hits the back of your head. Was it a policeman's club or another rock? You feel blood running down your back from the wound on your head. Everything gets fuzzy as you fall to the sand. The next time you open your eyes, you're in the hospital. Your head aches, but you're grateful to be alive.

THE END

To follow another path, turn to page 11.
To read the conclusion, turn to page 101.

Stylish young women in Washington, D.C., watched a football game.

CHAPTER 3

WORDS OF HARLEM

It's hard to believe that you are really a college graduate. You're the first girl in your family to go to college. Howard University in Washington, D.C., has been your home for the last four years.

At first you were amazed at the idea of a black university. You had never been surrounded by so many smart and ambitious people. Now it's 1925, and the studying is over. But where should you begin your new life?

Your parents want you to return to Memphis, Tennessee. Your family has lived there for generations. Memphis isn't bad, but you're not sure you want to go back yet. Many of your friends are moving to Harlem, in New York. That's where everything is happening.

Turn the page.

A student worked in a laboratory at Howard University.

Maybe one of your professors, Alain Locke, can give you some advice. You've also heard that a family friend, Ida Wells-Barnett, is in town giving a lecture. It would be nice to see her and hear any advice she might have.

→ To listen to Ida Wells-Barnett's lecture, go to page 43.

→ To visit Alain Locke, turn to page 45.

The lecture hall is filled, so you stand in the back. Ida Wells-Barnett was born a slave in 1862. She became a teacher and attended Fisk University in Nashville, Tennessee. Her life as a crusader started in 1884. She bought a first-class train ticket to Nashville, but the white conductor tried to force her into another car. It took three men to drag her out of the car.

The incident made her so mad that she started writing newspaper articles about how blacks were treated unfairly. She became part owner of a black Memphis newspaper, the *Free Speech and Headlight*. When a friend was hanged by a lynch mob, she wrote anti-lynching articles that angered local whites. A mob broke into the newspaper offices and destroyed the printing press. From then on, she fought for the rights of black Americans.

Turn the page.

"Those men threatened to lynch me," Ida is saying. "My friends wrote me desperate letters, begging me not to go back to Memphis. They said there were orders to shoot me on sight. An armed gunman was in the train station to meet every train from the North, just in case I was on it."

After the lecture, Ida spies you in the crowd. She gives you a hug and asks about your parents. Ida listens as you ask for advice about your future.

"Harlem is exciting!" she says. "You could do great things if you went there." She pauses. "But the renaissance, as they're calling it, isn't just happening in Harlem. There are changes going on everywhere. Even in Memphis. You could do a lot of good back home too. Don't let the bright lights of New York blind you."

➻ To move to Harlem, turn to page **48.**

➻ To return to Memphis, turn to page **70.**

Professor Locke leads you into his office. "The up-and-coming poet of campus. I remember your work," he says. "So good to see you again."

It's flattering that he remembers the poems you wrote for class. But that's not why you're here. He listens as you explain your problem.

"You're part of the Talented Tenth," Locke says. "You're educated and driven. You, and other New Negroes, can be leaders. But mainly that means you have the power to make real changes."

"New Negroes?" You've never heard that term before.

Locke smiles. "It's a term I like to use. The New Negro Movement is all about pride, self-confidence, and throwing off the shackles of the past. It's part of this renaissance for black Americans, writers, artists, and thinkers."

Turn the page.

He digs through the clutter on his large desk and pulls out a magazine. "I edited a special edition of the *Survey Graphic* this year," he says proudly. He flips the magazine open to a page of poetry and pushes it to you. You read:

Bring me all your dreams,
You dreamers,
Bring me all your heart melodies
That I may wrap them in a blue-cloud cloth
Away from the too-rough fingers
of the world

"Langston Hughes wrote that," Locke says. "Another bright new writer I know." He leans forward and says he understands your wish to go back to Memphis.

Langston Hughes helped invent jazz poetry.

"But Harlem is humming with a life that you won't find anywhere else," he says. "It's filled with every kind of person. The air vibrates with possibility. You have a real talent for writing. Grab it and own it. The chance may never come again."

You lay awake all night thinking. By dawn you've made your decision.

→ To move to Harlem, turn to page **48**.

→ To go to Memphis, turn to page **70**.

New York, here you come! Professor Locke is happy with your decision. He even writes you a letter of introduction to W.E.B. DuBois, editor of *The Crisis*. *The Crisis* is an important magazine for black Americans.

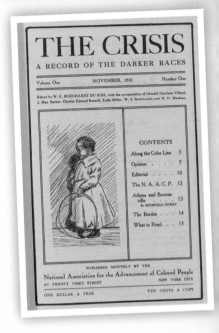

There are so many jobs in Harlem, you hear, that you'll have no trouble finding one once you're there. Then you'll have plenty of money for an apartment.

You want to arrive in New York in style. You have just enough money for a first-class train ticket. But if you buy a regular ticket, you'll have more spending money when you get to Harlem.

→ To buy a regular ticket, go to page **49**.

→ To buy a first-class ticket, turn to page **51**.

No sense wasting money on a first-class ticket. You board the train and settle in. Passengers are still boarding when the conductor approaches you.

"May I see your ticket, please?" he asks. He stares at it a moment.

"You'll have to come with me," he says. You ask him why.

"There's been some, um, complaints," he says. You're confused. You haven't done anything except take your seat. The other passengers, all white, watch. No one moves to help you. Then you understand. It's because you're black.

"I have paid my ticket!" you say loudly. "I have a right to be here!"

"You have to ride elsewhere," the conductor says angrily. "There's a place in the baggage car for you."

Turn the page.

"I will not ride in the baggage car like a stowaway," you argue, trying to keep your voice level. "I paid for my ticket."

Two other conductors appear. You're surrounded.

"Very well," you say, picking up your bags. You get off as the train starts pulling out of the station. It takes everything you have not to cry.

At the ticket window you ask for a refund. The woman behind the counter shakes her head. "You voluntarily got off the train," she says. "No refund."

Giving up, you sink onto a bench. It will take weeks to save enough money for another ticket. Maybe your parents will help. But for now your dreams of joining the Harlem Renaissance will have to wait.

THE END

To follow another path, turn to page 11.
To read the conclusion, turn to page 101.

You could get used to this, you think as you settle into the first-class compartment. The plush seats are comfortable. White-gloved waiters serve delicious food on china plates. You read the kind letter Professor Locke wrote to introduce you in New York.

He also gave you the name of Zora Neale Hurston. She went to Howard too, but she left last year. From the way Professor Locke tells it, Hurston is going to take the Harlem literary world by storm one day. You hope she can help you find a place to stay.

Turn the page.

When the train arrives in New York, you're excited. The bustle and noise of the big city is so amazing! The morning sun shines on the tall buildings, making the steel glow. It's still early. You could go to *The Crisis* offices and meet Mr. DuBois. Or you can find Hurston.

→ *To go to* **The Crisis** *offices, go to page* **53.**

→ *To look for Hurston, turn to page* **58.**

You're at 69 Fifth Avenue, the offices of *The Crisis* and the National Association for the Advancement of Colored People (NAACP). A well-dressed man sits at one of the larger desks. "Mr. DuBois?" you ask. He smiles.

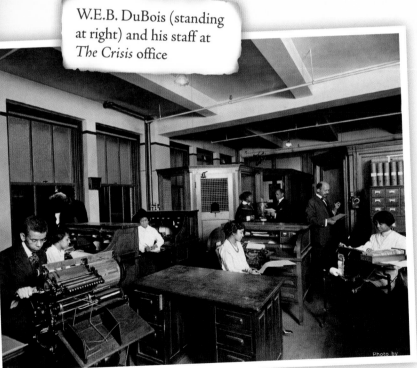

W.E.B. DuBois (standing at right) and his staff at *The Crisis* office

Turn the page.

"Ah, you must be the young poet Alain spoke about," he says, motioning you to sit. "Forgive me, but we are on deadline. I'll be with you in a moment."

It's too much to believe that you're actually here, talking to the great W.E.B. DuBois. He's the first black person to receive a doctoral degree from Harvard University. He's one of the founders of the NAACP and has been the editor of *The Crisis* since 1910. He's written poetry, plays, and a book. He's also a respected teacher.

"Alain tells me you are quite talented," DuBois says. "He also tells me that you need a job. Have you ever worked for a magazine?"

You shake your head. DuBois peers at you through his glasses, then nods. "Well then, let's see what you can do. I have two jobs. The proofs for James Weldon Johnson's next article are ready to be delivered to him in Harlem. Or you can stay here and read some pieces that we might publish. If you do either of these things well, I may consider you for a job."

➼ To deliver the package to James Weldon Johnson, turn to page **56**.

➼ To read some stories, turn to page **64**.

James Weldon Johnson was one of the leaders in the NAACP.

You can't believe that DuBois trusts you with such an important errand. Johnson is one of the most famous writers of the renaissance. You read his books *Fifty Years and Other Poems* and *The Book of American Negro Poetry* in college. But you know him best from his song "Lift Every Voice and Sing." You've sung it since you were a child. It's known as the Black National Anthem now.

"Johnson just moved into an apartment in Harlem," DuBois says. "Don't worry about bringing the proofs back today. Tomorrow is fine."

It's not hard to find the stately red building. A pretty woman answers the door, and you explain your errand. "I'm Grace Nail Johnson," she says. "Come in." James Weldon Johnson walks into the room. "Ah, I've been waiting for these," he says. Star-struck, you hand him the proofs.

"Tell DuBois I'll be around later," he says, smiling. "Thank you for coming all the way up here."

When you get back outside, you blink in the early afternoon sun. It's a warm day. You sit on a nearby stoop and look around. The address you have for Zora Neale Hurston is nearby. Suddenly you feel very tired. The long day of travel and excitement is catching up with you. And you don't have anywhere to stay tonight.

➤ To go to Hurston's home, turn to page **58**.

➤ To find a hotel for the night, turn to page **69**.

The door bursts open when you knock. An attractive woman looks at you. "Are you Zora?" you ask. Once you explain who you are, she smiles widely. "A Howard woman!" she exclaims, pulling you inside the fashionable apartment. Jazz music drifts from a phonograph machine. Zora introduces Countee Cullen and Langston Hughes. "I call our little group the Niggeratti," she explains as she hands you a cold drink.

Zora Hurston beat a drum called a hountar.

She sees the shock that crosses your face, and she laughs. "Yes, I know how most people use that word. But it's our way of owning it, making it powerful. We're the smartest, most talented, and amazing young black artists in Harlem. And I'm their queen!" Everyone laughs.

"Do you have a place to stay?" Hurston asks. It's embarrassing to admit that you don't. "Nonsense," she says. "You can stay here until you find your own apartment. We're all off to the *Opportunity* awards dinner tonight. You can come with us or stay here and rest."

⇝ *To stay at Hurston's home, go to page* **60**.

⇝ *To go to the awards dinner, turn to page* **61**.

After everyone has left, you collapse. But the music coming from the street below is too inviting. So are the delicious smells from the restaurants that line the street. You stroll up the street. You take in the well-dressed crowds and the packed sidewalks. Laughter fills the air. You're finally here. You can call Harlem home.

60

THE END

To follow another path, turn to page 11.
To read the conclusion, turn to page 101.

Your tiredness vanishes as soon as you walk into the Fifth Avenue Restaurant. This is the most amazing restaurant you've ever seen. More than 300 people fill the room. The women are dressed in elegant gowns. The men all wear tuxedos. You find a seat with Hurston. You spot Professor Locke and James Weldon Johnson in the crowd.

"Everyone wants to win an *Opportunity* prize," Hurston says. "I'm up for a prize, and so is Countee and Langston."

When the prizes are announced, you're delighted that Zora wins second place for her short story. Countee Cullen wins second prize for a poem called "To the One Who Said Me Nay." Then James Weldon Johnson stands up and reads Langston Hughes' first-prize poem, "The Weary Blues."

Turn the page.

The CRISIS

APRIL 1923

15 cents the copy

The Crisis is still published by the NAACP.

After dinner the conversation steers toward you and your future. "What do you plan to do here in Harlem?" Hughes asks. "The sky is the limit for those willing to work hard. Tonight is a good example of that!"

"I'm really hoping to get a job at *The Crisis*," you reply. "I love writing, especially poetry."

"There's always room for another poet—especially one with something important to say," Hughes says. "I'd be happy to help you if I can."

You can't believe your good fortune. You feel right at home with your new friends. You're so happy you decided to come along with Hurston to the awards. Maybe your dream of becoming a published poet will become a reality sooner than you even hoped.

THE END

To follow another path, turn to page 11.
To read the conclusion, turn to page 101.

"Jessie, my dear," DuBois calls to a woman across the room. She smiles and offers her hand. "I'm Jessie Fauset," she says.

You're impressed. Jessie Fauset is the literary editor of *The Crisis*. Her novel, *There Is Confusion*, was your favorite when it was published last year. Since she began working at the magazine in 1919, it has published some of the best Harlem Renaissance writers.

Jessie Fauset was a gifted student and taught French and Latin before coming to *The Crisis*.

She hands you some papers. "Read this story, then tell me what you think," she says. "It's part of a book that one of my writers, Claude McKay, is working on."

Soon you're lost in the story, which is set in Harlem. One passage jumps out at you. It's a description of Harlem in the spring:

The lovely trees of Seventh Avenue were a vivid flame-green. Children, lightly clad, skipped on the pavement. Light open coats prevailed and the smooth bare throats of brown girls were a token as charming as the first pussy-willows.

"He makes Harlem feel so real and alive," you tell Jessie.

She nods. "He has a gift. I hope his book gets published. It's called *Home to Harlem*. Claude is living in Europe right now. Maybe one day he'll come home.

Turn the page.

Claude McKay wrote four novels as well as poetry.

"You know how to read with an editor's eye," she continues. "I could use a good assistant. Would you like the job?"

Just like that, and you're working on one of the most important black magazines in America! Your feet don't seem to touch the ground as you leave the office. Suddenly your stomach growls, and you realize how hungry you are. But you still need a place to stay.

66

➺ *To have dinner first, go to page* **67**.

➺ *To find a place to stay for the night, turn to page* **69**.

You find a small café and enjoy a wonderful dinner. After the meal you drag your luggage onto the sidewalk. A young, well-dressed man approaches you.

"Are you lost, miss?" he asks. "New in town?"

"Yes," you reply, relieved to see a friendly face. "Do you know of any hotels?"

"Of course," he smiles and picks up your bag. "There's one just a few blocks away. Follow me."

The man rounds the corner into a darkened street. He drops your bag and turns around. You gasp. He has a knife in his hand.

"All your money, if you please," he says. Trembling, you hand over your money.

"And the jewelry too."

Turn the page.

You don't move. There's no way you're going to give him your gold graduation ring, your great-grandmother's beautiful pearl necklace, and your amethyst hat pin. Swiftly you kick him, hoping to knock him down. Your aim is off and you knock his shin instead.

The thief lets out a yell. You feel a sharp pain in your side, then the rush of warm blood. He rips the jewelry off you and then picks up your bag. "I'm sure whatever is in here will be worth something," he says. Wiping the bloody knife on your new coat, he leaves as you crumple to the ground.

THE END

To follow another path, turn to page 11.
To read the conclusion, turn to page 101.

The sign for the Hotel Olga catches your eye. The rooms are small but clean. Most important, the hotel welcomes black people. You barely drop your bags before you head to bed.

The sounds of jazz music float up from the street below. Even though you're tired, the music pulls at you. The very air seems charged with music and excitement. Tonight the music of Harlem will put you to sleep. Tomorrow you will start your new life as part of the Harlem Renaissance.

THE END

To follow another path, turn to page 11.
To read the conclusion, turn to page 101.

Your parents are waiting as you step off the train. It's good to be back. Two days later your parents host a party in your honor. As the party is winding down, your father finds you. There's a gray-haired woman with him.

"There's someone I'd like you to meet," he says. "Julia Hooks, this is my daughter."

Julia Hooks was a talented piano player who also taught music classes.

You've heard of Julia Hooks all your life. She's a teacher, activist, and one of the founding members of the Memphis branch of the National Association for the Advancement of Colored People.

"I understand that you are looking for a job," Miss Hooks says. "Have you ever considered social work? There are good jobs for women like yourself helping our community."

You can't believe your good luck. Julia Hooks was a teacher and founded the Hooks Cottage School. She also started the Colored Old Folks Home and the Orphan Home Club and worked as an officer of the juvenile court. You never dreamed you'd work with someone as famous and respected as Julia Hooks. Coming home was the right decision.

THE END

To follow another path, turn to page 11.
To read the conclusion, turn to page 101.

Duke Ellington played piano with his band at the Cotton Club.

CHAPTER 4

MUSIC IN THE AIR

Living in Harlem was always your dream. When you studied art at Fisk University in Nashville, all everyone talked about was Harlem and the renaissance of black culture. You dreamed of becoming a famous artist in New York.

Unfortunately things don't always work out. You got a job in Harlem as a janitor at the National Urban League building. It paid the bills, so you didn't mind. You figured you'd soon be making your living as an artist.

Two years later it's 1927, and you're still a janitor. It feels like the renaissance is passing you by.

Turn the page.

A crowd gathered to enjoy jazz at the Savoy.

One of your friends published a book. Your pal Jimmy plays trumpet in a jazz band. But your dreams of becoming a famous artist are fading.

One afternoon Jimmy stops by your workplace. "My band is playing the Savoy tonight," he says excitedly. "See you there!"

The Savoy is the most popular ballroom in Harlem. You'd like to leave work now to get there before the crowds. But your boss would not be happy if you left early. But maybe it would be OK.

→To stay at work, go to page 75.

→To leave early, turn to page 77.

"You know the boss," you say sadly. "I'll come after I'm finished."

Cleaning the offices of *Opportunity*, the National Urban League's magazine, is your last chore. Most of the time there's nothing to look at except trash cans overflowing with paper. Tonight something catches your eye. It's a painting leaning against a wall. You're awed by the power of the black figures. The backgrounds are done in bold, strong lines.

"Do you like my painting?" a voice makes you jump. A young man about your age is standing behind you.

"Sorry to startle you," he said. "I'm Aaron Douglas. I had to drop this off today. It's going to be an illustration for *Opportunity*."

Turn the page.

Illustration! The idea of painting for a magazine had never occurred to you. When you tell Douglas that you're a painter, his eyes light up. "The editors are always looking for promising black artists," he says. "You should bring some samples in sometime."

After Douglas leaves, you rush to the basement. Your boss has let you use a corner as a painting studio. You change clothes and grab some of your paintings. But by the time you get back to the *Opportunity* office, your excitement is gone. The whole thing seems like such a long shot. There's no way a magazine as important as *Opportunity* would publish art by a janitor. Or would it?

➤ *To leave and meet Jimmy, go to page* **77.**

➤ *To drop off your work, turn to page* **82.**

The streets are jumping. The crowds surge along the sidewalk, heading for restaurants and clubs. Groups of beautiful girls wrapped in raccoon coats roam the streets. Tonight you're going to the Savoy. Ropes of electric lights make the sidewalk in front of the Savoy bright as day. You're almost to the doors when someone waves at you. It's Delores, a friend who's a dancer.

The Savoy became the most popular ballroom in Harlem.

Turn the page.

"Forget the Savoy. I'm going to the Cotton Club," she says. "Duke Ellington is playing tonight!"

"You can't go there," you gasp. "It's for whites only."

Delores sniffs. "Not the musicians, dancers, singers, and staff," she replies. "I'm going to sneak in the back and watch from the stage."

One of the best things about the Savoy is that it's integrated. It's the only place in New York where blacks and whites can dance and have fun together. But Duke Ellington is a big deal.

➤ To go into the Savoy, go to page **79.**

➤ To go with Delores to the Cotton Club, turn to page **93.**

"No, I promised Jimmy," you say. "Besides, I feel like dancing tonight!" Delores can't be convinced to join you, and she leaves.

There's no place like the Savoy. The building is as long as a city block! The best bands in New York play here. The music is pumping, and the floor is filled with people stomping and swirling. One corner is reserved for the best dancers.

Jimmy is already onstage, wailing away on his trumpet. You wave and then look around for a dance partner. The place is filled with pretty girls. A black girl in a red coat smiles at you. A white girl in a sparkly dress catches your attention too.

➤ To ask the girl in the sparkly dress to dance, turn to page **80**.

➤ To ask the girl in the red coat to dance, turn to page **84**.

This is the first time you've ever danced with a white girl. Her name is Betsy, and she lives downtown. She's a good dancer. Jimmy's band is on fire tonight. The polished wooden floor bounces under the feet of 3,000 dancers.

After a few songs, you thank Betsy for the dances and go to find something cold to drink. It's hot in the ballroom, so you duck outside to cool off. You're in an alley with a few others who came out for some air.

Beautifully dressed dancers made a night at the Savoy a special event.

Three white men appear in the alley. "My buddies here say you were dancing with my sister," the biggest one says. "You dirty—"

The door bursts open, and three bouncers surround you. They're all ex-boxers, big and mean. The white men back away and disappear.

"Thanks," you say as everyone goes back in the club. Betsy finds you and apologizes for her brother. You don't feel like talking to her, even though none of this was her fault. "I think I'll call it a night," you say.

By the time you get back to your apartment you're too tired to care about what happened. You do know one thing. You had a great time, and you'll do it again.

THE END

To follow another path, turn to page 11.
To read the conclusion, turn to page 101.

Nothing ventured, nothing gained. You scrawl a quick note on your paintings and leave them on top of the desk. As you turn to leave, an angry voice yells, "Stop!" Aaron Douglas stands there with another young man.

"What are you doing?" the man says.

"Wait, Eric, he's the one I was telling you about," Douglas says.

"I see," the man replies. "I thought you might be trying to steal something. My apologies." He looks at the paintings. His anger turns to surprise.

"These are quite good," he says admiringly. You tell him that you studied at Fisk University.

"Is that so," he says. "The former editor of *Opportunity*, Charles Johnson, just accepted a position at Fisk. I'm the contributing editor and business manager here. I'm Eric Walrond."

Charles S. Johnson was the first black president at Fisk University.

Walrond picks up your work. "May I keep these?" he asks. "I can't promise anything, but I think you're very talented. There may be a job here for you."

Walking out with Douglas and Walrond feels great. It's the chance you've been waiting for. You hope it's the start of your new career.

THE END

To follow another path, turn to page 11.
To read the conclusion, turn to page 101.

"My name's Amelia," the girl says as you guide her through the crowd. Jimmy's band starts a fast-paced jazz number. Amelia is a great dancer. Soon you're spinning her all over the dance floor. Some of the dancers are doing a new step you've never seen.

New dances were created during the Harlem Renaissance, including the Lindy Hop.

"It's the Lindy Hop," Amelia says. "It was invented here at the Savoy. It's named after Charles Lindbergh, the pilot, and his famous transatlantic flight." She shows you the steps. You've never had so much fun.

You and Amelia dance all evening. Jimmy finds you at closing time as you're getting your coat. He presses a card into your hands. It's an advertisement for a rent party tonight. It claims that Fats Waller will be there!

"This is going to be a great party," he says. "Let's go."

"I can't," Amelia says. "I need to get home."

➻ To walk Amelia home, turn to page 86.

➻ To go to the rent party with Jimmy, turn to page 88.

The evening is perfect for a walk. The streets are still filled with people, even at this hour. Soon you get to Amelia's block. You're trying to decide whether to kiss her good night when you hear shouts. A group of teenage boys are scuffling in the street.

"That's my brother Thomas," Amelia says worriedly. "Those bullies have been bothering him for weeks."

Without thinking, you dash down the street. The rest of the group is pounding a thin boy wearing glasses. One by one, you pull each bully off and toss him into the street.

"Get out of here, and don't come back," you growl. "If you ever bother this guy again, you'll have to answer to me."

The boys know a threat when they hear it. They jump up and scatter. Amelia helps her brother to his feet. Thomas looks embarrassed but grateful.

"How about I teach you a few boxing moves," you offer. "Next time you can surprise them." Thomas grins.

So does Amelia. She gives you a quick peck on the cheek. "See you soon," she says with a big smile.

THE END

To follow another path, turn to page 11.
To read the conclusion, turn to page 101.

The party is in an apartment building near the Savoy. Rents are so high in Harlem that people either share an apartment or throw rent parties to raise money.

Everyone has to pay a dollar to get into this party. Usually it's just a dime or a quarter. But Fats Waller, the best piano player in Harlem, is going to perform. He grew up here and learned to play piano when he was a kid. He's known all over the world.

Fats Waller played the organ as well as the piano.

It's already hot and crowded when you get there. Delicious smells waft from the kitchen. Jazz music blares from a small radio. All the furniture in the apartment is gone. The only thing left is a piano in the middle of the front room. Jimmy's chatting with a pretty girl in a blue satin dress. Everyone drinks, eats, and dances for hours. The crowd erupts in cheers as Fats Waller ambles in. You want to meet him more than anything.

The room is really hot, and you're very thirsty. Jimmy hands you a glass of clear liquid.

→ *To drink it, turn to page* **90**.

→ *To put it down, turn to page* **91**.

You swallow the drink in one gulp, then sputter and gag. "What was that?" you gasp. Jimmy grins. "Bathtub gin," he says. "It's about time you tried it."

It's not long before your stomach is churning. The music is suddenly too loud, and the crowd is too close. Stumbling out the door, you sink onto the floor. The hall tile feels cool. If the world will stop spinning, you could get home. You hope Jimmy won't leave you here when he goes home.

Staggering to your feet, you make it to the street below. Two blurry figures appear. One pushes you against a wall. The other goes through your pockets. Your head is spinning and you can't fight back. With a laugh, one punches you in the face. Blood spatters on the sidewalk as you fall to the ground.

90

THE END

To follow another path, turn to page 11.
To read the conclusion, turn to page 101.

Wrinkling your nose, you put down the glass. That's bathtub gin. Since alcohol was outlawed in 1919, people make homemade liquor. There's no telling what is in this drink. It could be rubbing alcohol mixed with flavorings. You're not going to find out.

Fats Waller thumps the keys, and the room explodes in cheers. In time, you're so tired from dancing, you can't move another muscle. Grabbing a glass of water, you stumble out into the hallway. Soon Waller comes out to stand with you.

Waller wipes the sweat off his forehead with a handkerchief. You offer him your water, and he gulps it down.

"A year ago, I was playing in Chicago," Waller begins. "Suddenly some guy stuck a gun in my stomach! He hustled me into a limousine. I thought I was a goner."

Turn the page.

"What happened?" you ask.

"He took me to another saloon, pushed me to the piano, and ordered me to play. When I looked out into the audience, I figured it out. Know who was there?"

You shake your head, fascinated.

"Al Capone, the famous gangster," Waller said. "It was his birthday. His boys kidnapped me so I could play for Capone. I was his birthday present."

Waller hands the glass back. "Rent parties are a lot safer," he says, and you both laugh. Waller goes back to the party.

You just met Fats Waller. Nothing will top that! It's time to go home.

THE END

To follow another path, turn to page 11.
To read the conclusion, turn to page 101.

The Cotton Club is the most famous nightclub in Harlem, but you've never been inside. You and Delores walk past the growing line of richly dressed white people waiting to get inside. You duck around the corner in a side alley and through a small door.

It's a madhouse backstage. Tall dancers and musicians in tuxedos dash past burly movers lifting and carrying equipment. A beautiful woman in costume glides past and gives Delores a smile.

"That's Adelaide Hall," Delores gasps. You've never heard of her. "She's a fantastic singer," Delores explains. "She's been in two or three Broadway shows. I hear she's going to star in a new one next year, called *Blackbirds of 1928*. She sings with Duke Ellington. I'll bet that's why she's here tonight."

Turn the page.

The Cotton Club was one of the most popular nightclubs in Harlem.

Before you can stop her, Delores disappears into the crowd, following Hall. You've got to find her before anyone realizes you've sneaked in. At that moment a familiar face walks by. It's Duke Ellington! The show is about to start, and you don't want to miss it.

→ To watch Duke Ellington, go to page 95.

→ To follow Delores, turn to page 96.

When the applause starts you run through the backstage and out to the waiter's station. All of the waiters and hostesses are black, so you're less likely to be noticed. Duke Ellington strides out, dressed in a tuxedo. The first burst of music almost blows you off your feet. You lose yourself in the music until someone grabs your elbow.

"Who are you?" From the look of his tuxedo, he is the head waiter. "I could get fired if anyone catches you here!" He makes a small motion and instantly two bouncers are on either side of you.

"Go quietly so we don't have to rough you up," one says. They toss you out a back door into the street. Your night at the Cotton Club is over.

THE END

To follow another path, turn to page 11.
To read the conclusion, turn to page 101.

"Delores, wait!" Your voice is drowned out by the noise backstage. You push your way past beautiful dancers in glittery costumes. You finally find Delores in a dressing room no bigger than a closet. "Come here!" she says, spying you. "Adelaide, this is the friend I was telling you about."

"Imagine my surprise to see Delores," Adelaide says. "We've been to so many auditions together!"

"And I would have been hired here at the Cotton Club if I'd been exactly 5 feet 6 inches tall!" Delores says. They both laugh.

"I must go on soon," Hall says. "After the show I'm having a few friends over for a quiet, late supper at home. Would you care to join us?" The last thing you want is to be quiet. But Delores clearly wants to go, and you shouldn't leave her behind.

➤ To leave the Cotton Club, go to page 97.

➤ To stay, turn to page 98.

It's late as you leave the club. You wish you could find Jimmy and the rent party, but you have no idea where it is. Finally you hear the sounds of music and laughter coming from a building. As you climb the stairs, two men burst out of an apartment. One throws a bottle at the other. He ducks, and the bottle shatters on your head.

When you wake, you're in a hospital. "The guy who hit you tried to dump you on the street," a nurse says. "Someone noticed and called the police. Get some sleep. You can go home in the morning."

So much for not being quiet, you think as you drift to sleep. No one realizes how badly you've been hurt. During the night, you slip into a coma. You never wake again.

THE END

To follow another path, turn to page 11.
To read the conclusion, turn to page 101.

You're hungry, and you've missed the first half of Duke Ellington's performance anyway. Adelaide shoos you and Delores out of her dressing room. The two of you wait outside the club until Adelaide finally comes out. A car and driver pull up to the curb. The three of you climb in.

Chorus girls danced during the Cotton Club's popular floor show.

Hall's large apartment is tastefully furnished. Soon people from the Cotton Club begin to arrive. Most of them are Delores' friends, but you don't know anyone. Just as you think you might die of hunger and boredom, one more guest arrives—Duke Ellington!

After the meal Ellington ambles to the piano and begins to play. Adelaide Hall leans in and whispers, "Duke likes to try out his new music first. You're hearing songs no one else has ever heard before."

Delores slides a friendly arm through yours. "What do you think of this 'quiet supper' now?" she teases.

You are so happy you came to the party. What a night in Harlem!

THE END

To follow another path, turn to page 11.
To read the conclusion, turn to page 101.

A couple danced the jitterbug at a Harlem club.

CHAPTER 5

A BRIGHT LIGHT, FADING AWAY

The Harlem Renaissance sprang to life after World War I ended in 1918. For years it felt like one big party. Millions of people left farms and small southern towns. They moved north to find a better life. People had good jobs and plenty of money to spend.

The 1920s were a blur of music, art, writing, and theater. Magazines published work from talented writers. Claude McKay and Jessie Fauset published important novels about black life. Duke Ellington and Fats Waller transformed music, bringing new jazz to the world. Josephine Baker and Adelaide Hall took the theater world by storm. Racial barriers seemed to matter less.

Turn the page.

It all came tumbling down in 1929. The stock market crashed in October. In an instant, thousands of people lost everything they had. Within two years millions of jobs were gone. Desperate, hungry people stood in bread lines or sold apples on the streets. The Great Depression had begun.

The Great Depression was the beginning of the end of the renaissance. Many of the artists and writers of the renaissance lost their regular jobs as maids, elevator operators, janitors, or waiters.

People waited in a bread line in New York City.

During the renaissance it was popular for wealthy white people to visit Harlem clubs, restaurants, and theaters and to sponsor black artists. After the crash people could no longer afford that kind of entertainment. The businesses closed, putting black workers out on the streets. Many black artists moved to Europe, where there was much less racism. Big organizations like the NAACP and the National Urban League stopped promoting the arts. Instead they focused on issues like jobs and poverty.

Harlem was hit hard. Half of all the families in Harlem were out of work. It was difficult for blacks to get government relief jobs because of discrimination. Property values dropped. Overcrowding and sickness made things worse. In 1935 rioters rampaged through Harlem, causing more than $200 million in damage.

A few artists managed to survive. Duke Ellington went on to become a legend in the music world. Langston Hughes became one of the best-known black writers. Adelaide Hall had a successful singing career. The NAACP and National Urban League still exist today.

Most renaissance figures faded away or died in the 1930s and 1940s. Zora Neale Hurston's best work, *Their Eyes Were Watching God*, was published in 1937. She kept writing novels, teaching, and traveling, but money was always a problem. In 1950 she was working as a maid. She became penniless and died in a welfare home in 1960. Jessie Fauset wrote four successful books: *There Is Confusion*, *Plum Bun*, *The Chinaberry Tree*, and *Comedy, American Style*.

The 20th annual session of the NAACP in Cleveland, Ohio, in 1929

Fauset later became a teacher and died in 1961. Claude McKay moved around the country and died in Chicago in 1948. James Weldon Johnson died in the 1930s.

The renaissance was about embracing black culture and being proud of its roots. The renaissance showed the world black life, culture, and sophistication. After the renaissance it became easier for black artists to be taken seriously for their work. More colleges and universities opened their doors to black students. Even though Harlem was ground zero for the renaissance, the power of these new ideas spread around the world.

Timeline

1909—National Association for the Advancement of Colored People (NAACP) is founded.

1910—W.E.B. DuBois founds *The Crisis*.

1911—National Urban League is founded.

1914—World War I begins.

1916—The Great Migration begins.

1917—The first of nearly 368,000 black soldiers are drafted into military service during World War I.

James Weldon Johnson publishes *Fifty Years and Other Poems*.

1918—The 369th Regiment is awarded the Croix de Guerre with silver star, France's highest military honor.

1919—Race riots break out in many communities in the United States.

1920—W.E.B. DuBois writes of the "renaissance of American Negro literature."

1921—*Shuffle Along* is one of the first all-black musicals on Broadway; an unknown dancer, Adelaide Hall, is in the chorus.

1923—The magazine *Opportunity* is founded.

The Cotton Club opens.

1925—Winners of the *Opportunity* literary awards include Langston Hughes, Zora Neale Hurston, and Countee Cullen.

1926—The Savoy Ballroom opens.

1927—Duke Ellington begins performing at the Cotton Club.

1928—*Blackbirds of 1928*, starring Adelaide Hall, opens on Broadway.

Claude McKay publishes *Home to Harlem*.

1929—The stock market crashes October 29.

1935—The Harlem Race Riots occur.

OTHER PATHS TO EXPLORE

In this book you've seen how the events of the past look different from three points of view. Perspectives on history are as varied as the people who lived it. Seeing history from many points of view is an important part of understanding it.

Here are some ideas for other points of view to explore:

+ Many people who moved to Harlem during the Great Migration were from the rural South. Running water, electricity, and cars were new to them. Contrast their lives in New York with how they lived in the South. (Common Core: Key Ideas and Details)

+ Being a black woman in the 1920s was doubly difficult. They faced racism because of their color and discrimination because they were women. Colleges that accepted black men, for instance, often did not accept black women. How did the shifting attitudes of the Harlem Renaissance help black women? (Common Core: Craft and Structure)

+ During the Harlem Renaissance, many black stereotypes were shattered. Black writers told stories about their lives that showed the world they were like everyone else. How would that affect white people's opinions about black people and their culture? (Common Core: Integration of Knowledge and Ideas)

READ MORE

Fradin, Judith, and Dennis Fradin. *Zora! The Life of Zora Neale Hurston*. Boston: Clarion Books, 2012.

Hill, Laban Carrick. *Harlem Stomp! A Cultural History of the Harlem Renaissance*. New York: Little, Brown, 2003.

McKissack, Lisa Beringer. *Women of the Harlem Renaissance*. Minneapolis: Compass Point Books, 2007.

Schroeder, Alan. *In Her Hands: The Story of Sculptor Augusta Savage*. New York: Lee and Low Books, 2009.

INTERNET SITES

Use FactHound to find Internet sites related to this book. All of the sites on FactHound have been researched by our staff.

Here's all you do:
Visit *www.facthound.com*
Type in this code: 9781476502564

GLOSSARY

boll weevil (BOHL WEE-vuhl)—an insect pest that feeds on cotton plants

discrimination (dis-kri-muh-NAY-shun)—treating people unfairly based on their race, country of birth, or gender

jazz (JAZ)—a lively, rhythmical type of music in which players often make up their own tunes and add new notes in unexpected places

Jim Crow (JIM KROH)—discrimination against blacks by rules and laws

lynching (LIN-ching)—putting to death, often by hanging, by mob action and without legal authority

migration (mye-GRAY-shun)—movement of people from one area to another

racism (RAY-siz-uhm)—the belief that one race is better than another race

regiment (REJ-uh-muhnt)—a large group of soldiers who fight together as a unit

renaissance (REN-uh-sahnss)—a time of great revival of art and culture

BIBLIOGRAPHY

Brown, Lois. *Encyclopedia of the Harlem Literary Renaissance.* Facts on File, 2006. 16 May 2013. www.scribd.com/doc/61368841/Encyclopedia-of-the-Harlem-Literary-Renaissance

Ferguson, Jeffrey. *The Harlem Renaissance: A Brief History with Documents.* New York: Bedford/St. Martin's Press, 2008.

Hutchinson, George, ed. *The Cambridge Companion to the Harlem Renaissance.* London: Cambridge University Press, 2007.

In Motion: The African-American Migration Experience. The Schomburg Center for Research in Black Culture. 16 May 2013. www.inmotionaame.org/print.cfm;jsessionid =f830185427134851348O379?migration=8&bhcp=1

Lewis, David Levering. *When Harlem Was in Vogue.* New York: Penguin Books, 1997.

National Urban League. 16 May 2013. http://nul.iamempowered.com/who-we-are/mission-and-history

Watson, Steven. *The Harlem Renaissance: Hub of African American Culture 1920-1930.* New York: Pantheon Books, 1995.

Wintz, Cary. *Black Culture and the Harlem Renaissance.* Houston: Rice University Press, 1988.

INDEX